First Facts®

Spiders

Tarantulas

by Molly Kolpin

Consultant:
Pedro Barbosa, PhD
Department of Entomology
University of Maryland, College Park

CAPSTONE PRESS
a capstone imprint

First Facts is published by Capstone Press,
151 Good Counsel Drive, P.O. Box 669, Mankato, Minnesota 56002.
www.capstonepub.com

 Books published by Capstone Press are manufactured with paper
containing at least 10 percent post-consumer waste.

Library of Congress Cataloging-in-Publication Data
Kolpin, Molly.
  Tarantulas / by Molly Kolpin.
    p. cm.—(First facts. Spiders)
  Includes bibliographical references and index.
  Summary: "A brief introduction to tarantulas, including their habitat, food, and life
cycle"—Provided by publisher.
  ISBN 978-1-4296-4520-1 (library binding)
  1. Tarantulas—Juvenile literature. I. Title. II. Series.
  QL458.42.T5K65 2011
  595.4′4—dc22

                              2010002254

Editorial Credits
Lori Shores, editor; Veronica Correia, designer; Eric Manske, production specialist

Photo Credits:
Alamy/Dan Morris, 21; David Haynes, 7; Rick & Nora Bowers, 20
James P. Rowan, 19
Minden Pictures/Heidi & Hans-Juergen Koch, 6
Nature Picture Library/Wegner/ARCO, 11
Newscom, 8
Pete Carmichael, 5
Peter Arnold/Biosphoto/Borrero Juan Manuel, 13; Meul, J., 15
Shutterstock/Justin Black, cover; Rich Lindie, 16; worldswildlifewonders, 1

Essential content terms are **bold** and are defined at the bottom of the page
where they first appear.

Printed in the United States of America in North Mankato, Minnesota.
012011   006038VMI

Table of Contents

Supersized Spiders

Tarantulas are the largest spiders in the world. Like all spiders, they have two main body parts. But unlike other spiders, these **arachnids** are about the size of a human hand.

Goliath birdeaters are the biggest tarantulas. With their eight legs stretched out, these spiders are about the size of dinner plates!

arachnid—an animal with four pairs of legs and no backbone, wings, or antennae

abdomen

cephalothorax

Mexican flame knee tarantula

Spider Fact!

When threatened, some tarantulas rub their legs together to make loud hissing noises.

Helpful Hairs

Thin, spiky hairs cover a tarantula's body. Some tarantulas flick hairs at enemies. The hairs make people itch and can kill small animals.

Columbian brown giant tarantula

flying hairs

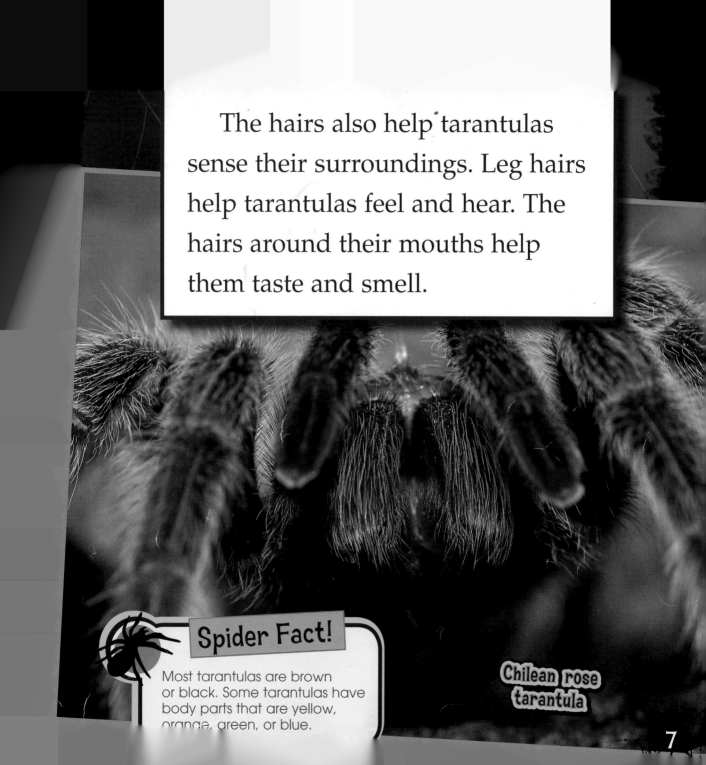

The hairs also help tarantulas sense their surroundings. Leg hairs help tarantulas feel and hear. The hairs around their mouths help them taste and smell.

Spider Fact!

Most tarantulas are brown or black. Some tarantulas have body parts that are yellow, orange, green, or blue.

Chilean rose tarantula

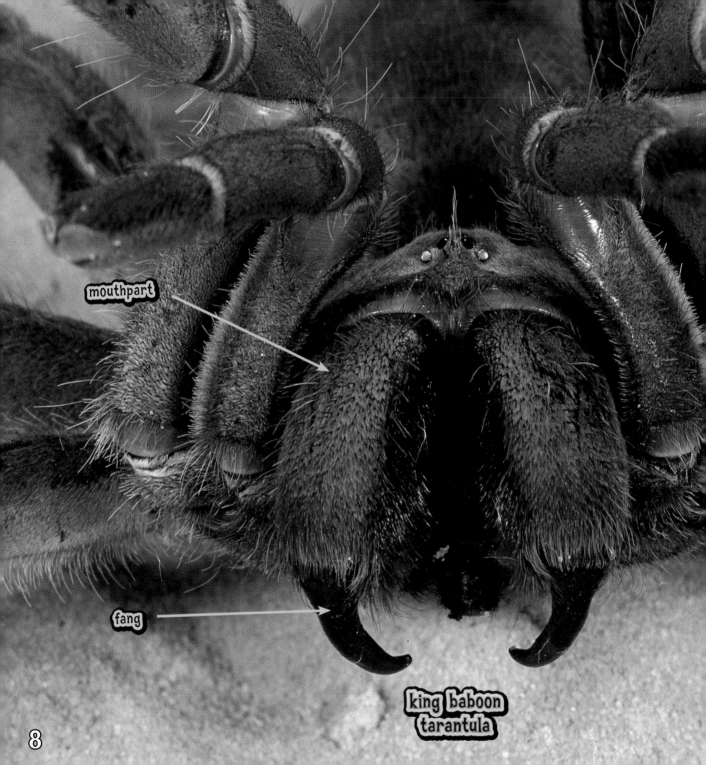

mouthpart

fang

king baboon
tarantula

8

Fearsome Fangs

Tarantulas have two large, sharp **fangs**. Their fangs can be up to 1 inch (2.5 centimeters) long. When not being used, the fangs are protected inside two large mouthparts.

Spider Fact!

Tarantulas show their fangs when threatened.

fang—a long, pointed toothlike mouthpart

When tarantulas bite, **venom** runs through their hollow fangs. The venom is strong enough to kill small **prey**, but not people. Tarantula venom is only as strong as the venom in a bee sting.

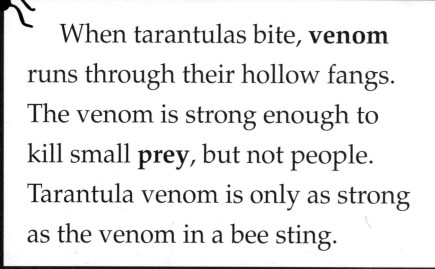

Spider Fact!

The tarantula's name comes from an old dance called the Tarantella. People thought this dance protected them against spider venom.

venom—a harmful liquid produced by some animals
prey—an animal hunted by another animal for food

Brazilian pink
tarantula

Tarantula Homes

Tarantulas live in warm places all over the world. Some live in wet rain forests. Others live in dry deserts.

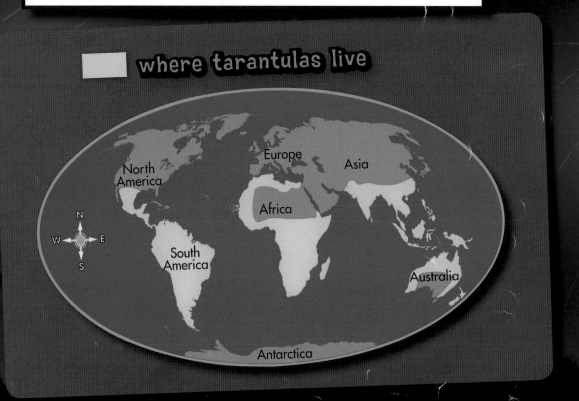

where tarantulas live

North America

Europe

Asia

Africa

South America

Australia

Antarctica

N W E S

burrow

Most tarantulas live in underground **burrows**. Some tarantulas make their homes high up in trees. Sharp, gripping claws make tarantulas good climbers.

Spider Fact!

There are about 850 kinds of tarantulas in the world.

burrow—a tunnel or hole in the ground where an animal lives

Spider Silk

Tarantulas don't build webs, but they still make **silk**. Many tarantulas line their burrows with silk. When prey walks by, the ground moves enough to shake the silk. Then the tarantula can rush out and pounce on the prey.

Spider Fact!

A piece of spider silk is stronger than a piece of steel that is the same size.

silk—a string made by spiders

huahini
birdeater

silk

15

Ecuadorian woolly tarantula

Spider Fact!

Some tarantulas can live for one year without food.

Big Eaters

Hungry tarantulas snatch bugs, mice, or frogs that walk past their burrows. Other tarantulas hunt for food at night. Large tarantulas even catch snakes and birds.

Tarantulas squirt juices into the prey's body to soften it. Then they suck up the mush through strawlike mouthparts.

Tiny Tarantulas

Male and female tarantulas mate to produce young. Then the female lays 75 to 1,000 eggs. She wraps the eggs in an **egg sac**. Tiny **spiderlings** hatch from the eggs six to nine weeks later.

The spiderlings stay near their mother for a short time. Then they leave to make their own homes.

Spider Fact!

Female tarantulas sometimes eat their own spiderlings.

egg sac—a small pouch made of silk that holds spider eggs
spiderling—a young spider

Life Cycle of a Tarantula

Newborn

Tarantula spiderlings are often carried on their mother's back.

young tarantula

Young

Tarantulas shed their outer skeletons many times as they grow.

Adult

Female tarantulas live for 25 to 30 years. Males live only five to 10 years.

Wicked Wasps

A tarantula's worst enemy is the tarantula hawk wasp. The female wasp stings a tarantula so it can't move. Then the wasp lays an egg on the spider. When the young wasp hatches, it eats the still-living tarantula!

Amazing but True!

People around the world eat tarantulas. In Cambodia, fried tarantulas are a popular snack. In a village in Venezuela, people use fangs as toothpicks after eating spiders. Some people say tarantulas taste like crunchy peanut butter.

Glossary

arachnid (uh-RACK-nid)—an animal with four pairs of legs and no backbone, wings, or antennae

burrow (BUHR-oh)—a tunnel or hole in the ground where an animal lives

egg sac (EG SAK)—a small pouch made of silk that holds spider eggs

fang (FANG)—a long, pointed toothlike mouthpart

mate (MATE)—to join together to produce young

prey (PRAY)—an animal hunted by another animal for food

silk (SILK)—a string made by spiders

spiderling (SPYE-dur-ling)—a young spider

venom (VEN-uhm)—a harmful liquid produced by some animals

Read More

Bredeson, Carmen. *Hair-shooting Tarantulas and Other Weird Spiders.* I Like Weird Animals! Berkeley Heights, N.J.: Enslow Publishers, 2010.

Camisa, Kathryn. *Hairy Tarantulas.* No Backbone! New York: Bearport Publishing, 2009.

Ganeri, Anita. *Tarantula.* A Day in the Life: Rain Forest Animals. Chicago: Heinemann Library, 2011.

Internet Sites

FactHound offers a safe, fun way to find Internet sites related to this book. All of the sites on FactHound have been researched by our staff.

Here's all you do:

Visit *www.facthound.com*

Type in this code: 9781429645201

Index